TO

_____

FROM

_____

DATE

_____

Seven-Minute Morning Journal

WAKING UP ISN'T ALWAYS EASY. There are a lot of unknowns outside that bedroom door, and if you're not careful, the day gets spent (along with your energy) without any real investment being made into what you know matters most.

So how do you greet the sunrise with more intention, hope, and expectation? It begins by waking up to the beautiful reality that your Creator knows you intimately, loves you passionately, and promises to stay with you relentlessly throughout every moment of your life. When you begin each day reflecting on His grace and refreshing your soul with the life-giving power of His Spirit, you can tackle whatever comes your way with a deeper sense of confidence and divine purpose.

This journal is your daily invitation to greet God each morning. May you gain precious insight from each devotional and divine inspiration as you meditate on each Scripture. Together may they help you wake up to each new morning with joy and hope, relishing His great love, reveling in His mercies, and receiving the power you need to live each day to its fullest.

the

Seven-Minute
Morning

JOURNAL

Inspiration for Your Quiet Time with God

DaySpring

LIVE YOUR FAITH

Stepping Out

Be strong and courageous. Do not be afraid or terrified because of them, for the LORD your God goes with you; He will never leave you nor forsake you.

DEUTERONOMY 31:6 NIV

LYDIA WAS A SUCCESSFUL BUSINESS OWNER in the male-dominated Roman Empire. A dealer of purple cloth in Thyatira, Lydia was not unique in her trade but certainly a pioneer in her personal life. She took Paul and Silas in after they had been jailed, she made the leap of faith to embrace Christianity, and her house may have served as a center for Christian work. Each of these decisions were risky on her part but also part of the entrepreneurial spirit she surely possessed.

Being brave requires faith, and having faith requires bravery. What does the Bible urge us to do, again and again, in the face of fear? To trust in the Lord. God has given each of us the capacity for bravery. But true, godly bravery means living according to what God alone tells us. This means putting our faith in God and putting His plans first, above anything else.

Your own version of brave probably doesn't look the same as anybody else's. A big presentation may scare some and thrill others. Being vulnerable with a friend may be overwhelming to one, while another might thrive on those raw, relationship-building moments. Being courageous is about stepping into your moment and away from anything that would distract you from God's plans for your life.

These days, every friend, family member, or follower has an opinion on what you show the world. But when one individual steps into their calling with courage, they pave the way for others to follow. An act of courage is a bold move forward that, even if uncomfortable at first, can lead to the best possible outcomes for your life.

What might courage look like for you today?

_____
_____
_____
_____
_____
_____
_____
_____
_____
_____
_____
_____
_____
_____
_____

God, my prayer today is...

_____
_____
_____
_____
_____
_____
_____

The Power of Prayer

I cried out to the LORD; yes, I prayed to my God for help.
He heard me from His sanctuary.

PSALM 18:6 NLT

THE GAP BETWEEN OUR LIPS and God's ears is the shortest distance in all of creation. And not only does God hear us, but I John 5:14–15 reminds us that when we ask according to His will, we will receive what we've asked for. When we say, "God, I want to make a decision in this situation that honors You." Or when we ask, "Father, comfort my friend as she deals with this horrible diagnosis," we know that these prayers are answered because our requests are aligned with God's will. We cry out, God hears, and He sees to it. We can place our needs in His hands and know that our prayers are more effective than any other earthly thing we can do.

Prayer is not a last resort. It's a first line of defense for anything you might go through. Perhaps this is a reason we sometimes wake up in the middle of the night for no apparent reason. It's an opportunity for God to have you all to Himself, inviting you into the very important habit of praying at all times. There's not much else to do at two o'clock in the morning, after all! Quiet your heart, ask the Lord why you're awake, and then pray about whatever comes to mind. There's literally no better investment you could make. And in the morning, thank God for being with you night and day.

What do you think it means to pray
without ceasing (1 Thessalonians 5:17)?

_____
_____
_____
_____
_____
_____
_____
_____
_____
_____
_____
_____
_____
_____
_____
_____

God, my prayer today is...

_____
_____
_____
_____
_____
_____

Real Rest

God gives rest to His loved ones.

PSALM 127:2 NLT

IT'S A FAIR ASSUMPTION that God pulled out all the stops while creating the world. And at the end of that week, after placing every strand of cheetah fur, causing water to fall over rocky cliffs, and breathing language into whales, He rested (Genesis 2:3).

The Hebrew word for rest in the Creation story outlined in Genesis is *shabath*, which literally means "to stop." When we think of rest, we tend to think in terms of relaxation. We crash on the couch, scroll social media, or watch an entire series of some show. Simply put, though, resting means ceasing. No worrying. No trying. Just trusting. Being still. Knowing that God is in control.

Rest is a conscious, waking activity. From the moment our eyes open in the morning, we can focus on things that are true, right, lovely, noble, and pure (Philippians 4:8). We can savor the moment, which may mean looking out the window near our desk and enjoying the sunny blue (or cloudy gray) sky. It might mean considering the intricacy of our child's face or the ring of our spouse's laugh. We can give worries to God. We can do the simple act of stopping, sitting, letting our minds wander, and enjoying the moment. What do you think God was doing after creating the world? Probably admiring its incredible beauty. You can do the same. Sleep may be for nighttime. But resting is for now.

What are some ways you may try to shabath today?

_____
_____
_____
_____
_____
_____
_____
_____
_____
_____
_____
_____
_____
_____

Father, my prayer today is...

_____
_____
_____
_____
_____
_____
_____

Hearing God's Voice

All your children will be taught by the LORD,
and great will be their peace.

ISAIAH 54:13 NIV

WHEN BABY PENGUINS ARE BORN, their ears are calibrated to the unique frequency created by the sound of their mom and dad's voices. This isn't just a handy thing for around the penguin neighborhood, or because to the human eye all penguins look alike! Penguin parents must leave their chicks, along with all the other chicks, to go hunt for food. Imagine the chaos when all the penguin parents come back to the newly born chicks, searching for their little guy in the huddle! Imagine the hubbub when hundreds of nearly identical black-and-white squawkers start hollering for their baby Henry. "Hey! Over here! No, over here! No, not that one! Wait, are you Henry? No? Have you seen him? He's gray, and little, with soft feathers..." That's why each penguin parent has its own unique vocal frequency. And why the baby learns it quick.

When penguin parents return to their young, they only need to call out. And among all the other families, the parents and babies find each other.

As humans, we each have our own unique DNA. And amazingly, we come pre-wired to know our heavenly Father's voice. It may look and sound different to us than to anyone else on the planet. But the imprint God gives us is recognizable to us—that's a promise.

How do you best "hear" God in your life?

_____
_____
_____
_____
_____
_____
_____
_____
_____
_____
_____
_____
_____
_____
_____
_____

God, my prayer today is...

_____
_____
_____
_____
_____
_____
_____

Hide in His Tower

The name of the LORD is a strong tower;
the righteous run to it and are safe.

PROVERBS 18:10 NKJV

THOUGH YOU'VE SLEPT FOR HOURS, you feel like your head just hit the pillow. Already your mind is swirling with thoughts for the day. Of course, there's the usual getting ready, making coffee, facing traffic. But there's more weighing on your mind than the daily grind. That conversation you had with your spouse the other night just didn't sit right. Your baby only says three words, and the milestone says it should be ten. There's a boss to please and laundry to fold, bills to pay and church to attend. You start to feel like you should just hide somewhere and hope everything works out.

God says His name is a strong tower, and the righteous run to it and find safety. He assures us that no one who comes to Him for protection will be turned away. He is our fortress, our secret place where we can hide, and He Himself will fight the big and small battles we face each day. There is no better place to go than to the only One with the power to save you in this moment, and your lifetime.

God doesn't want us to tuck Him into a corner and visit Him when it's convenient. He wants to fill every room, every space with an unwavering hope that only He can give. So hang out in that tower called His Name. It will be a safe, warm, and comforting refuge in everything you do.

What is making you feel like hiding this morning,
and how can you surrender it to God?

_____
_____
_____
_____
_____
_____
_____
_____
_____
_____
_____
_____
_____
_____

Lord, my prayer today is...

_____
_____
_____
_____
_____
_____
_____

Surprise Yourself

"For I know the plans I have for you," declares the LORD...
"plans to give you hope and a future."

JEREMIAH 29:11 NIV

HAVE YOU EVER TRIED a new hobby that you ended up being really good at? Archery for example—a bull's eye, or close to it, on your first visit to an archery range? Or what about playing the guitar or baking a cake? Chances are, you weren't worried about how you'd do on your first try. You were probably surprised and happy that you were able to accomplish something new with positive results. You may have been encouraged to try again and maybe even continue learning that craft or skill.

Billions and billions of people have gone before you, trying and failing and succeeding, over and over again. The amazing humans in your life now are the result of hundreds of generations of people doing their very best to live with strength and joy. In fact, you are too! And most importantly: God is there to lead, show grace, forgive, refine, and help—every step of the way. When we choose Jesus, we also receive the gift of the Holy Spirit to be the still, small voice who guides us. And that means in the big and the little, you and the Lord will make good decisions together.

The bottom line is, don't be afraid. Trust your gut. Trust in God. You'll most likely surprise yourself with what you can accomplish when you put all you have in His hands.

What new things might you try today?

_____
_____
_____
_____
_____
_____
_____
_____
_____
_____
_____
_____
_____
_____

God, my prayer today is...

_____
_____
_____
_____
_____
_____
_____

Worry-Free Living

Seek first His kingdom and His righteousness,
and all these things will be given to you as well.
Therefore do not worry about tomorrow.

MATTHEW 6:33-34 NIV

AS WE READ and rely on Scripture, one thing we can be sure of is that if God commands it, He makes it possible. When He commands us to seek His kingdom above the world's "treasures," that means there's a kingdom of heaven available for us to discover. When He commands us not to worry, then He gives us the ability to not worry as we lean on Him. Sounds and feels impossible at times, doesn't it?

Fortunately, God provides tools to help us in this battle of the mind. Isaiah 26:3 tells us that as we keep focused on God, He keeps us in peace. Second Corinthians 10:5 gives us the action step of taking our negative, worrisome thoughts captive—not allowing them to sabotage our peace. John 15:1-11 gives us the simple yet very challenging task of resting in Him in order to obtain the fruit of peace.

Wondering how to quit worrying? Try presenting your requests to God by prayer, with thanksgiving (Philippians 4:6). Thank Him for your beautiful family, warm home, or the gift of music. As you focus your attention on the good of His kingdom, He will lift your eyes above the mess and help you observe the world from His perspective—a very peaceful perspective.

*Are you carrying a worry this morning? If so, are you ready
to lay it down and start the day fresh?*

_____

_____

_____

_____

_____

_____

_____

_____

_____

_____

_____

_____

_____

_____

God, my prayer today is...

_____

_____

_____

_____

_____

_____

Happy or Blessed

How happy is anyone who has put his trust in the LORD.

PSALM 40:4 CSB

PEOPLE DON'T ALWAYS ASSOCIATE the words *happy* and *blessed* as synonyms. It's possible to know God has blessed you without feeling happy; likewise, happiness sometimes feels fleeting or different from what we normally associate with being blessed by God.

But what if happiness is more than an emotion based on our circumstance? What if we can receive happiness as readily as we can lift an Amazon package off the porch, open it up, and enjoy the fruits of one-day shipping? What if happiness is actually a blessing from God? And what if true, godly happiness is the kind of gift that reveals itself only as the recipient invests?

Imagine you've got a pocket full of nickels and you want a soda, which costs two dollars in the vending machine. You begin inserting nickels into the slot. It takes a while, but you keep investing until the bottle tumbles down. You trust that soda will come because that's what a vending machine is designed to do.

What if happiness works the same? We make deposits of trust in God every day. And we begin to enjoy happiness as a way of life. The more we trust—the more we thank Him, pray, and worship Him—the happier we become. Our investments of trust, in a sense, allow Him to give us more and more satisfaction in Him and His ways.

What are you trusting God with today?
Do you feel happy or blessed or both today? Explain.

_____

_____

_____

_____

_____

_____

_____

_____

_____

_____

_____

_____

_____

God, my prayer today is...

_____

_____

_____

_____

_____

_____

_____

Comforting Connection

He will cover you with His feathers,
and under His wings you will find refuge.

PSALM 91:4 NIV

DID YOU KNOW THAT SKIN TIME (diapered baby on mama's bare chest) can regulate a newborn's own body temperature? If the baby is cold, mama can warm her. If the baby is too hot, mama can cool her, regardless of mama's own temperature.

God, in all His greatness, holds us as close as a newborn on a parent's chest. In Psalm 139:10, it is His right hand that keeps us close. In Psalm 91, we are tucked into His feathers. In Psalm 27:10, God ensures us that His willingness to hold us in His arms is even more powerful than our own parents' love.

When all else fails, a sincere hug will speak volumes. In the middle of the night, when bad dreams or fevers or teething interrupts sleep, your arms will be the comfort your child needs. When a spouse or a friend is struggling, a sincere touch can remind them they're not alone. Holding a hand can mirror God's love to someone who needs just a touch of reassurance. Take courage in the fact that sometimes all your loved ones need is to feel you physically close while God does the rest. Your touch is a tool that will keep you connected.

Are you comfortable with using gentle touch
as a ministry of God's love?

_____
_____
_____
_____
_____
_____
_____
_____
_____
_____
_____
_____
_____
_____

God, my prayer today is...

_____
_____
_____
_____
_____
_____
_____

A Loving Helper

I will send you the Helper from the Father;
He is the Spirit of truth who comes from the Father.

JOHN 15:26 NCV

WITH GOD, YOU ARE ENOUGH. With God on your side, you were made for this life. You do not have all the answers, nor do you need to! You are fully equipped to do today. You are equipped because God gives you everything you need.

In many areas of life there are good practices and lots of good paths to the same solution. It's up to you and God to do your journey in the way that builds your relationship with Him.

In John 15:26, Jesus promised to send the Holy Spirit to lead us in the truth. Step by step, He helps us to discover our values and desires as believers in Him. This helps us choose our paths each day. After all, He knows us and our circumstances better than anyone else. He knows when we need to step out boldly or take it slow. He knows when we should keep moving forward on our current path and when we should try something brand-new. And He has the very best in mind for each of us.

There's no need to be overwhelmed by social media or the opinions of others. Listen to your Helper, tune in or tune out according to His suggestions, and get ready for a blessed life with Him.

How has God been your Helper in the past?

_____
_____
_____
_____
_____
_____
_____
_____
_____
_____
_____
_____
_____
_____

Lord, my prayer today is...

_____
_____
_____
_____
_____
_____
_____

Winning the Race

Press on toward the goal.

PHILIPPIANS 3:14 NIV

CLIFF YOUNG WAS A 61-YEAR-OLD POTATO FARMER who entered the Sydney ultramarathon in 1983. He'd spent his life chasing after sheep, sometimes running two or three days to catch them all. So five days wouldn't be that different, he said. That was the amount of time expected for this 544-mile race.

At the end of the first day, Mr. Young, wearing his everyday overalls, was so far behind that he had no idea the other runners actually stopped to sleep for six hours, or that it was expected he would do so too. He carried on. For five days. He ran without stopping. And he ended up beating the other competitors by ten hours. His approach of nonstop jogging put him two days ahead of the previously held ultramarathon record in Australia.

Like Mr. Young, today is the beginning of a journey you've trained for solely by living your life. You've shown up in your street clothes and can only imagine what lies in store for you. But also like Mr. Young, you don't need to run fast. Just keep putting one foot in front of the other. Wash the dishes, again. Feed and burp and change, again. Try, dream, play, get up when you fall, make music, and smile at strangers. Start a project. Finish a task. Hug your spouse. Agonize and imagine and pray and love. Always love.

Life is full of moments that seem to offer no reward. But the prize comes at the end when God acknowledges you and blesses you for living and loving so well.

What is your favorite mundane task, and why?

_____

_____

_____

_____

_____

_____

_____

_____

_____

_____

_____

_____

God, my prayer today is...

_____

_____

_____

_____

_____

_____

_____

A Fearless Future

I will go before you and level the uneven places.

ISAIAH 45:2 CSB

LET'S FACE IT: Worrying is easy. Everyone does it! We can set out intending to give everything to God and live a worry-free day—just as He says we're capable of in His Word—but at some point we're bound to start wandering through the "what if's" about something we can't control. And soon enough, we're back to worrying.

When things of the future get scary, remind yourself of Isaiah 45:2: God promises to go before you and level out the uneven places. He will make a way forward. That doesn't mean life will be perfect and painless. But God does promise to go with you (Exodus 33:14). He promises never to leave you, never to forsake you (Hebrews 13:5). He promises that if you seek Him, He will be found (Jeremiah 29:13).

God promises that if you pray and ask, then His peace (the kind that it doesn't make sense to have, considering the circumstances) will guard your heart and your mind in Christ Jesus (Philippians 4:6-7). When your mind starts going down the path that leads to worry, then speak to your mind. Remind it that all those things you're imagining haven't happened, and they most likely will never happen. But whatever does happen, God will give you the grace for it. And He'll go through it with you. You truly can be present without fearing for the future.

What worries can you give to God today? How does it
make you feel to know that God will never leave you,
no matter what comes your way?

_____
_____
_____
_____
_____
_____
_____
_____
_____
_____
_____
_____
_____

Father, my prayer today is...

_____
_____
_____
_____
_____
_____
_____

Love Songs

The LORD your God is in your midst. . . .
He will rejoice over you with joy,
He will be quiet in His love.

ZEPHANIAH 3:17 NASB

THE SECOND IT COMES ON THE RADIO, your heart soars—it's your all-time, hands-down favorite love song. Without a second thought, you crank it up in your car loud enough to be heard from outside, but inside you've let the music and melody take you where it always does, to that special place in your mind. You imagine another place and time where you reveled in the affection and attraction of some significant other, a place where you were free to not only be yourself but to be fully loved as the quirky and unique person you are. For the three minutes the song plays, you are in your perfect paradise.

Of course, when the song ends, the day's realities resume. And romantic notions of hope and deep connection get shelved for another day, perhaps another song. In real life, your experience tells you that even the best, most enduring loves might not last, at least not with the unbridled passion of youth. In real life you have to settle for a love that's more, well, down to earth. Or do you?

Maybe that's exactly the problem with an earthbound love. We were made for more. We were designed to know and be known at the deepest levels of our soul. Did you know that the God who created you sings love songs over you as well? His commitment to you has no rival. He alone can satisfy your aching soul with the kind of connection you truly crave. Unlike love songs on the radio, God's singing for you started before He made the world, and His delight in you doesn't fade away. It welcomes you to stay in His presence and revel in His love now and forever.

How will you revel in God's love for you today?

_____
_____
_____
_____
_____
_____
_____
_____
_____
_____
_____
_____
_____
_____

God, my prayer today is...

_____
_____
_____
_____
_____
_____

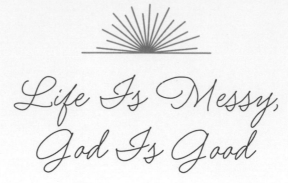

Life Is Messy, God Is Good

You shall love the LORD your God with all your heart,
with all your soul, and with all your strength.

DEUTERONOMY 6:5 NKJV

THE LITTLEST THINGS can throw us way off our game, can't they? We may have planned our day to a tee, only to spill coffee on our lap at breakfast and watch the entire plan go up in smoke. It happens to all of us! Fortunately, we have a God who understands. He knows that without His mercy, we would widely miss the mark of perfection.

Once, Jesus was asked the question, "Teacher, which command in the Law is the greatest?" (Matthew 22:36 CSB). Jesus responded by saying, "Love the Lord your God with all your heart, with all your soul, and with all your mind. This is the greatest and most important command. The second is like it: Love your neighbor as yourself" (Matthew 22:38-39 CSB).

When the rubber meets the road, remember this: You are loved. You have God's mercy on your side. And if you simply love Him back, with everything in you, then He'll lead you through all the messes of life—the ups and downs and sideways, as well as the unknowns and unseens. Keep it simple, and let God handle the rest.

How are you going to handle the messes of life today? What's
your plan for when things don't go exactly right?

_____

_____

_____

_____

_____

_____

_____

_____

_____

_____

_____

_____

_____

_____

God, my prayer today is...

_____

_____

_____

_____

_____

_____

_____

Fashioned by Design

It's in Christ that we find out who we are and what we are living for.
Long before we first heard of Christ and got our hopes up,
He had His eye on us, had designs on us for glorious living,
part of the overall purpose He is working out
in everything and everyone.

EPHESIANS 1:11–12 THE MESSAGE

YOU ARE NOT AN ACCIDENT or a mistake. There is nothing about you that is generic or derivative or "mass-produced." No, you are a true masterpiece, unique and one-of-a-kind, fashioned by design. Beautifully handcrafted by God Himself. Every detail is exquisite, purposeful, and deliberate. Your personality and temperament, background and life experiences, gifts and talents—all these things make you, you. All these things make you—and you alone—perfect for the plan God has for you. Embrace this truth!

Celebrate your true beauty, a reflection of your Creator's beauty. Use it to help others discover His beauty—and their own.

What are some characteristics you like about yourself?
How does God use these to bring light to the world?

_____

_____

_____

_____

_____

_____

_____

_____

_____

_____

_____

_____

_____

Lord, my prayer today is...

_____

_____

_____

_____

_____

_____

A Good God

O taste and see that the LORD is good.

PSALM 34:8 KJV

GOD IS FULL OF GOODNESS. When we have the chance to experience Him in our lives, it's the taste we remember and want for as long as we live. We may not recognize that that's what we need. We may not know where to find it, especially on challenging days. But the goodness of God is what fills us, prepares us, and makes us able to thrive.

Life is literally overflowing with opportunities to taste the goodness of God. Sometimes those moments are obvious—like warm hugs, big accomplishments, and joyful laughter. Other moments are more like an acquired taste. It can be hard to recognize through fevers or fights. But there is always something worth savoring. How? Through thankfulness. Even the act of waking up in the morning is a gift worth thanking Him for. We can thank Him for health, for enough food, for heat or air conditioning. It's different for everyone. But every time we acknowledge those little morsel moments of goodness in our days, it gets easier and easier to see how rich our lives truly are.

Name three examples of God's goodness you see right now...

_____
_____
_____
_____
_____
_____
_____
_____
_____
_____
_____
_____
_____
_____
_____

Father, my prayer today is...

_____
_____
_____
_____
_____
_____

The Grace We Need

Because of His great love for us...
God raised us up with Christ and seated us
with Him in the heavenly realms.

EPHESIANS 2:6 NIV

EPHESIANS 2:6-7 OFFERS a one-of-a-kind promise: a seat with Jesus in the heavenly realms, so that "He might show the incomparable riches of His grace (verse 7 NIV)."

This promise means that Jesus leads us to a place far above our current circumstances. We might be experiencing heavy or multiple challenges—but at the same time, we can lean on Him to lift us up and show us the bigger picture. By faith, we have all the grace we need to get through any challenge. With His help, an explosive argument can turn into a bonding experience. Money trouble can turn into a sweet time of prayer and a chance to empathize with others. The next new thing to worry about can become a chance to release it to God and watch Him lead you through.

It can be so hard to remember this good news when you're suffering through. You can do some things in less stressful times to help yourself out when it's tough. A sticky note on the edge of your windshield can draw your eyes upward. Dry-erase notes on your mirror, asking an accountability partner to memorize Ephesians 2:6 with you, and regularly thanking God are all great strategies. And of course, when you're struggling, simply asking Him to show you the heavenly perspective can change your outlook in just a moment.

What sort of reminders can you put into place today to remind you of His grace when you need it most?

_____
_____
_____
_____
_____
_____
_____
_____
_____
_____
_____
_____
_____
_____

Lord, my prayer today is...

_____
_____
_____
_____
_____
_____
_____

On Earth As in Heaven

Your kingdom come. Your will be done
on earth as it is in heaven.

LUKE 11:2 NKJV

NOT SURE HOW TO PRAY? What to say? What to expect, hope for, ask, or want? Often we know what we *don't* want. We also want to see a situation resolve in the way God would choose. So, how do we line ourselves up with His heart?

There's no clear definition in the Bible of God's will. We often pray, "If it's your will," but without an understanding of what that means, isn't it a little bit of a guess? Perhaps the closest thing to a definition of God's will comes in what we call The Lord's Prayer (found in Matthew chapter 6 and Luke chapter 11): "Your will be done on earth as it is in heaven." *On earth as it is in heaven.*

Is there sickness in heaven? Pray against sickness on earth. Are there broken relationships in heaven? Pray for relationships to heal on earth. A mother learns during labor that the umbilical cord is wrapped around the baby's neck and the baby is in danger. There is no physical harm in heaven, so she prays for the baby's safety. If we're wondering how to pray for our current situation, we need only to look as far as God's kingdom.

Jesus is always the best example for how to operate. He was in touch with His Father, so His prayers were always answered. As you begin the day, be encouraged by the way Jesus operated, and know that you can pray for the very best. Right here, as it is in heaven.

What does "on earth as it is in heaven" mean to you?

_____
_____
_____
_____
_____
_____
_____
_____
_____
_____
_____
_____
_____

God, my prayer today is...

_____
_____
_____
_____
_____
_____

In Love with You

No power in the sky above or in the earth below—
indeed, nothing in all creation will ever be able
to separate us from the love of God
that is revealed in Christ Jesus our Lord.

ROMANS 8:39 NLT

NO MATTER HOW WELL we do or do not measure up... God just keeps on loving us like He does. He actually enjoys us. He knocks on the door of our lives, and in some weird way, He delights in us. Here we are—people who routinely break His heart. We surely frustrate Him. We think we are little gods running the show. We misbehave. But He keeps on knocking on the door, keeps on loving us. That's the one thing we've all got to know.

The most liberating truth in all the universe is this: Jesus is absurdly in love with us. He is for us. He is for you! You might turn your back on Him, change your mind about Him, stomp your feet at Him, or run away from Him. But He will never, ever leave your side. You might fall, stumble, trip, fumble, sin, grumble, and make a general mess of things. But He can't not love you. He made a way back, a way up, a way out, and a way in. He came for you, all the way to earth, to rescue you. And He's not giving up on you now. Let God drop that truth into your heart. Hear Him tell you how He loves you with a reckless love. And nothing, absolutely nothing, can stand in the way of it.

Do you believe God loves you?

_____
_____
_____
_____
_____
_____
_____
_____
_____
_____
_____
_____
_____

Lord, my prayer today is...

_____
_____
_____
_____
_____
_____

Driving Lessons

Create in me a clean heart, O God.
Renew a loyal spirit within me.

PSALM 51:10 NLT

NOTHING SHINES A LIGHT on our shortcomings quite like traffic. Words are said, feelings felt, and maneuvers performed, that we would all be embarrassed by if we were just standing next to someone on the street.

Sometimes it seems easy to graciously let the driver in from the merge lane. We nod and smile at pedestrians in the crosswalk. Other times, we mutter unmentionables at the Kia with its blinker on in front of us or the verrrrry slow walker keeping us from turning right. Never mind when that other person does something that we find irritating. *Ugh, I thought I was turning more and more into a picture of Jesus.*

It's a wonder that throughout our lives, we fall back again and again into the thinking that we can do the hard work without God. Even when He's helped us a thousand times. We need His grace to give us what we're missing. And we need His mercy to free us from what holds us back. We need His healing touch to help us move on and His wisdom to know how to move forward. When little ones enlighten us to areas that need His touch, we need Him to do the work in us that He promised to do.

His work is expert. It's the path of least resistance. Really! We can try to kick a habit or adapt our methods. But only God can purify our hearts—the place where our attitudes, actions, and words are born.

When is your attitude most likely to be challenged?

_____
_____
_____
_____
_____
_____
_____
_____
_____
_____
_____
_____
_____
_____
_____
_____

Lord, my prayer today is...

_____
_____
_____
_____
_____
_____
_____

The Gift of Grace

*My grace is sufficient for you, for My strength
is made perfect in weakness.*

II CORINTHIANS 12:9 NKJV

I<small>T'S HIGHLY UNLIKELY</small> that there will ever be a time in life when the clouds part, the music soars and you'll think, *I've arrived! This is it! I have achieved perfection, ta-DAAAA!* No matter how hard you work, no matter how gentle or firm, scheduled or relaxed, consistent or gracious, fun-loving or militant you are, "arriving" in this life is impossible.

Thankfully, life doesn't require perfection. It requires grace. It can be hard to accept grace, either for yourself or for others, because in truth we don't deserve it. Grace is a gift from God, and for some reason it's difficult to accept free gifts when we realize how imperfect we really are. But as long as we accept Jesus, we can accept His gift of grace.

The funny thing about grace is, the more you realize you need it, the more you are able to give it to other people. Becoming a parent often softens our heart toward our own parents and the faults we perceived them as having. Anytime we need someone to give us the benefit of the doubt, we can see it as an opportunity to remember that others need the benefit of the doubt from us. From the perspective of the roller coaster called Life, we can more easily recognize when someone else is just trying their very best. And that is good enough, because grace covers us all.

When was the last time you needed someone to show you some grace?

_____
_____
_____
_____
_____
_____
_____
_____
_____
_____
_____
_____
_____
_____
_____

God, my prayer today is...

_____
_____
_____
_____
_____
_____
_____

It's Already Within You

*It is not that we are competent in ourselves
to claim anything as coming from ourselves,
but our adequacy is from God.*

II CORINTHIANS 3:4-5 CSB

WORRY IS A DRAIN on your precious reserves of time, energy, and emotional strength. How much better it is to talk those worries over with God and then let Him keep watch. You don't have to know everything there is to know—promise. God has placed certain instincts within you, instincts that surface once you relax and let them flow naturally. You're already more equipped than you think.

And it's important to remember that God made you. That's right, you are His creation, and He knows you inside out and backwards. When you need strength, He will bolster you. When you need insight, He's the fountain of all knowledge. Sometimes He will provide what you need by sending someone your way, and sometimes He will help you reach down deep inside and find what you need to get the job done.

Every single situation you face, no matter how it feels at the time, is an opportunity to look back on and cherish when you walk through it with God. You only get one life, and you'll only live today once. Be comforted by God's own Word, the Bible, and allow Him to help you enjoy every moment.

What are you looking forward to today?

_____
_____
_____
_____
_____
_____
_____
_____
_____
_____
_____
_____
_____
_____

Father, my prayer today is...

_____
_____
_____
_____
_____
_____

In This You Can Trust

Trust in Him at all times...
pour out your hearts before Him.
God is our refuge.

PSALM 62:8 CSB

IT'S NOT ALWAYS TOP OF MIND to turn to God in every circumstance...
but that's exactly what He hopes we'll do. Even on those days when all the
everythings are crumbling around you for no good reason... Chin up. Take
heart. Turn to God. Remember, He can be trusted.

God has equipped you for literally everything you'll come in contact
with today. If He hasn't equipped you for something, then He won't allow it
to come your way. In that you can trust.

Nothing happens that God hasn't foreseen. He's never knocked off-
balance by some unexpected drama. In that you can trust.

When you're aching, tired, lonely, scared, confused, and at your
wits' end...God is already there to comfort you and show you the way out.
Sometimes that just means a nap and a cup of coffee, and if so, then He's
already enlisted someone to make sure that happens for you. In that, you
can trust.

While He knows it all, God still wants you to tell Him. He makes space
for you to cry out to Him, simply so that He can show you how much He
cares. He wants to hear your heart.

No season lasts forever, even though there are moments it feels like
things will never change. And remember...no season lasts forever. These are
moments you will never get back. So trust God. At all times. Pour out your
heart and allow Him to be your refuge.

What can you trust God with today?

_____
_____
_____
_____
_____
_____
_____
_____
_____
_____
_____
_____
_____
_____

Lord, my prayer today is...

_____
_____
_____
_____
_____
_____
_____
_____

Choosing to Trust

*"I am the Lord's servant. May everything
you have said about me come true."*

LUKE 1:38 NLT

MARY WAS ENGAGED. She was a virgin. And she was pregnant. With the Messiah. As a devout Jewish girl, there was nothing usual—or acceptable—about her situation. "An angel said I'm carrying God's Son" probably didn't quell the angry rumors. Mary was most certainly surrounded by skeptics and furious family members. Not to mention a very confused Joseph, her fiancé.

But as far as the Bible reflects, Mary didn't allow her senses, or those of the people around her, to dictate her heart position. Her stance was to trust in the Lord, even when her circumstance—her situation—was intense. She chose to believe her God when He said it would all be okay.

Mary looked past her surroundings and made choices in line with God's heart for her, for His Son, and for the eternal story of His kingdom. To do this, she lived out Proverbs 3:5-6 on a daily basis: to trust in God, to rely on Him alone, to know the depths of His heart, and to let Him lead her. It was this lifestyle of intimacy with Him that allowed her a wise answer in the time of greatest need.

How does building a relationship of trust with God differ from going to Him just when you need Him?

_____
_____
_____
_____
_____
_____
_____
_____
_____
_____
_____
_____
_____

Lord, my prayer today is...

_____
_____
_____
_____
_____
_____

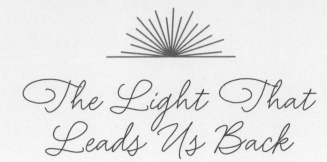

The Light That Leads Us Back

If anyone is in Christ, there is a new creation...
everything has become new!

II CORINTHIANS 5:17 NRSV

HAVE YOU EVER FELT LONELY? Most likely, we all have. Seems kind of crazy, knowing how busy we can all be with activities, responsibilities, and social media. Often though, those are just distractions from the fact of our loneliness. We use wine, online shopping, schedules, a paycheck, or food to fill our deep-down dissatisfaction. But loneliness isn't something you solve. Loneliness becomes the light leading us back to Jesus.

Through loneliness, God reveals to us all the ways we depended on our capacities instead of His grace. Our loneliness isn't lost on God; it's a means to form us into Christlikeness—so that we resemble Him more and more. God is growing you into a new creation, bending and breaking your character into deeper trust in His forever love.

Loneliness isn't to be feared, pushed aside, or pressed under. Feel its ferocious appetite and the ways you're tempted to fill that hole with anything and everything but God. Let love meet you in the middle of your vulnerable void. The void that Christ knows full well. The place where all the world's weight of loneliness pressed Him to pray, "Why, God, have You forsaken Me?"

Meet Christ right there, right where He is always meeting you—arms stretched wide, chest open, love mercifully exposed, welcoming you into a loneliness He fully understands. Your loneliness finds company with Christ. It leads us back to love.

How do you tend to distract yourself from loneliness?

_____
_____
_____
_____
_____
_____
_____
_____
_____
_____
_____
_____
_____

Father, my prayer today is...

_____
_____
_____
_____
_____
_____
_____

"I Knew You When..."

*I knew you before I formed you
in your mother's womb.*

JEREMIAH 1:5 NLT

MINUTES AFTER A BABY IS BORN, a nurse brings in an ink pad and document. She puts the baby's foot on the pad, then gently touches it to the paper. Later she hands the new mother a print of the baby's feet. They are marvelous. Their tiny size, perfect shape, and intricate creases are nearly impossible to comprehend.

Those prints—so special and detailed that not even an artist could recreate them—were hand-tooled by their Creator.

"You saw me before I was born. Every day of my life was recorded in your book. Every moment was laid out before a single day had passed." (Psalm 139:16 NLT)

"Even before He made the world, God loved us and chose us in Christ to be holy and without fault in his eyes." (Ephesians 1:4 NLT)

Footprints and fingerprints are daily reminders that God knows every single detail about us. He made the blueprints, designed the dream of us, and then molded us into the perfect little human forms that emerge into the world. God has a wonderful plan for each of us, even before we are born. And His indelible print is left on each of us, made in His image, and capable of more than we can imagine.

List a few ways you are unique from anyone else.

_____

_____

_____

_____

_____

_____

_____

_____

_____

_____

_____

_____

God, my prayer today is...

_____

_____

_____

_____

_____

_____

_____

They Come and Go beyond the Fire

Trials will show that your faith is genuine.
It is being tested as fire tests and purifies gold—
though your faith is far more precious than mere gold.

1 PETER 1:7 NLT

THE SEEDS OF A LODGEPOLE PINE are completely sealed with resin, which needs to be burned in order for the seed to be released and take root. If you were one of these seeds, you just might experience two different feelings when you got the first hint of smoke off in the distance. One: "Oh no, this will hurt!" And two: "Awesome, now I can pass my legacy on to the next generation!"

There will be days you just don't feel ready for anything. Sometimes we can kick ourselves out of a funk. And some days, all we can do is wait for bedtime and hope for better dreams than the realities of the day. No one loves being refined or challenged. But when we have faith in Jesus, we know that the fire of refinement leads to a much sharper, more beautiful view of the world.

It's good to remember that hard days will come. It's even better to remember that hard days will go. After all, you've made it through as many days as you've been alive. If you can hang onto the knowledge that every challenge is a chance for refinement and that you'll be passing a legacy of faith and growth on to those around you, then the hard days just might start bringing you a smile.

When was the last time you had a rough day?
Did you let it refine you somehow?

_____

_____

_____

_____

_____

_____

_____

_____

_____

_____

_____

_____

_____

Lord, my prayer today is...

_____

_____

_____

_____

_____

_____

Wait, Look, Trust

*My God will meet all your needs
according to the riches of His glory in Christ Jesus.*

PHILIPPIANS 4:19 NIV

GOD IS THE GIVER of every good gift, and He is very generous in His giving. There will never be a time, He says, when you'll lack exactly what you need. Sometimes that won't feel true—but in those moments we can dig a little deeper. Wait a little longer. Look a little harder. Trust a little more. His resources are always delivered right on time (though not always early enough for us to get too confident—because relying on Him is a gift in itself too).

In the dark of night, when your mind won't turn off: God is awake too. When worries and wonderings and struggling relationships bring tears to your eyes: God is aware. When friendships or bones get broken: God is a healer. When the unthinkable things, or the most wonderful things you can think of, fill your days: God is an unshakable presence, every step of the way. As you learn to tap into all that He is and all that He has for you, you become the confident child of God He's designed you to be.

What is one way God showed up for you recently?

_____
_____
_____
_____
_____
_____
_____
_____
_____
_____
_____
_____
_____

Father, my prayer today is...

_____
_____
_____
_____
_____
_____

God's Inscription

I, God, will never forget you. Look here.
I have made you a part of Me,
written you on the palms of My hands.

ISAIAH 49:15–16 VOICE

WHEN YOU WERE A CHILD, did your parents ever accidentally leave you at a mall or a restaurant? Was there a time when each thought the other had picked you up from school? Were you ever left off the invitation list to a special party? Ignored or overlooked by others at church or at work?

At one time or another, we've all experienced the pain of feeling abandoned, rejected, neglected, or unloved. The Bible describes a time when God's people felt that way. They thought that He had forgotten and forsaken them. But God said, "No way!"

He will never, ever let go of His people. He will never leave us or forsake us. In fact, He loves us so much that He has our names "inscribed" or "engraved" on the palms of His hands, where He will always see them and be reminded of how much we mean to Him. Those same hands are holding our hearts and lives today.

Do you feel safe in God's hands? Why or why not?

_____
_____
_____
_____
_____
_____
_____
_____
_____
_____
_____
_____
_____
_____
_____

God, my prayer today is...

_____
_____
_____
_____
_____
_____
_____

Expect the Very Best

Those who wait on the LORD shall renew their strength;
they shall mount up with wings like eagles,
they shall run and not be weary,
they shall walk and not faint.

ISAIAH 40:31 NKJV

ACCORDING TO WEBSTER'S 1828 DICTIONARY, to expect is to wait for or to look for something. The implication is that the "something" is definitely coming—something in the future, something already promised. God gives us dreams, plants the seeds, waters them with time and experience, and allows them to grow to maturity before releasing them into the world. He gives us the tools to live out the vision He has cast for us. We learn, we work with Him, and His glory is revealed.

Expect the very best from God in the coming months and years. Prepare yourself for whatever dreams He's been whispering into your heart: Clean up your schedule. Tell people you trust. Think hopefully and joyfully about what He's unfolding in and through you... He's been planning on this time in your life since before time began. In a way, as you wait on Him and expect His very best, He is waiting on you and expecting the great things He has already planned.

What dreams are you hoping for?

_____
_____
_____
_____
_____
_____
_____
_____
_____
_____
_____
_____
_____

God, my prayer today is...

_____
_____
_____
_____
_____
_____
_____

A New Way of Seeing

*Come to Me, all you who are weary
and burdened, and I will give you rest.*

MATTHEW 11:28 NIV

SOME SEASONS IN LIFE are just bound to break us down. Sometimes it's because our new circumstances take us by surprise. Other times, try as we might to prepare, we're just not ready for what comes our way. But if we let it, that breaking down can be a beautiful thing. We learn as we go. We make adjustments, cling to Jesus, surrender our control, and discover a new way of looking at what we have now.

Don't feel bad if you struggle with losses: lost free time, lost sleep, lost joy for a while. Loss is painful. Sometimes very painful. Because you cared, you grieve.

Also, don't feel bad if you don't master new skills or attitudes right away. We are human. Which means that we will be fighting imperfection our entire lives on earth. Instead, watch for the subtle changes. Trust the process of God at work in your life. Work hard to cultivate a sense of humor. And know that every minute, every day, the Lord is changing your heart more and more to reflect His own.

What "new" are you experiencing lately?

_____
_____
_____
_____
_____
_____
_____
_____
_____
_____
_____
_____
_____
_____

Lord, my prayer today is...

_____
_____
_____
_____
_____
_____
_____

Last and Least

The Lord says, "Bethlehem Ephrathah,
you are one of the smallest towns in Judah,
but out of you I will bring a ruler for Israel,
whose family line goes back to ancient times."

MICAH 5:2 GNT

WHEN SAMUEL ANNOUNCED that God had sent him to anoint Israel's next king, Jesse proudly produced all eight of his strapping sons, eager to see which God would choose. Well, seven. David was the eighth, the last and the least, and his own family completely forgot about him. No one bothered to call him in from the fields, where he was watching the sheep. They didn't think it was important; they didn't think he was important. But as God said no to brother after brother, it soon became clear: David was His choice.

Over and over in Scripture, God reminds us that He has a different standard, a different way of measuring things. And that there are no limits to what He can do. A heart like David's—a heart that fully belongs to Him—that's the most important thing. So God called David from the pasture to the palace, to rule as Israel's greatest king. And He made him part of Jesus's family tree.

How is God working in your life today?

_____
_____
_____
_____
_____
_____
_____
_____
_____
_____
_____
_____

God, my prayer today is...

_____
_____
_____
_____
_____
_____

Blazing Trails!

God is within her; she will not be toppled.

PSALM 46:5 CSB

WHEN YOU SAY YES TO GOD, you're saying yes to the most amazing, trail-blazing adventure ever. If you've ever watched a jungle adventure movie, you know that blazing trails can be scary! Monkeys and snakes can fall from the trees and attack. If tigers or gorillas find you in their territory, you're a goner. Poisonous plants and spiders are just waiting for you to get close. And never mind if you wander near the camp of a native warrior....

Okay, it's not THAT scary! But sometimes it feels as if we're ill-equipped to handle the territory we find ourselves in. Yet God is on our side, that's a promise. As our fortress, we have Him to rest in, hide behind, and call on. Trekking through the jungles of jobs, relationships, family, or big choices, God is the shade that protects us from slippery snakes or tricky tigers. When we stay under His covering, we learn to accept what details we can affect today and let the rest go. When constricting time wants to squeeze in, His schedule allows us to breathe and relax. God is our camouflage, allowing us to pass unscathed through worries and fears as we hand them to Him. And God's Word refreshes us and helps us keep a right perspective on the world.

Leaning on God as we go, we can't fail. Yes, we will fall. We will make mistakes. But we will get up again, and more likely than not, the good will far outweigh the hard.

What adventures are you going to take today?

_____
_____
_____
_____
_____
_____
_____
_____
_____
_____
_____
_____
_____
_____
_____

God, my prayer today is...

_____
_____
_____
_____
_____
_____
_____

How Are You?

From the end of the earth I will cry to You,
when my heart is overwhelmed;
lead me to the rock that is higher than I.

PSALM 61:2 NKJV

LIKE THE SPEEDOMETER and gas gauge in a car, feelings tell us when it's time to do something different. You drive until the gas light comes on, and you know that if you don't act fast, you'll be stuck on the side of the road. You watch the numbers on the speedometer, knowing if they exceed the sign you just passed, you might see flashing lights in your rearview. So you slow down.

Feelings are similar. You can be exceedingly happy, indicating that this is a moment to savor. You can be super sad, indicating that you could probably use a good cry and a good talk with someone. If you're angry and overwhelmed, it might just be time to step away for a minute and take a few deep breaths.

Absolutely no one can blame you for feeling a certain way. It's what you do about it in the moment that makes the difference. Adopt one or two plans for those moments when you need to take a breather. And always remember that God is just a breath away, waiting to comfort you and remind you that you're cut out for this adventure called life. Truly.

How are you feeling this morning?

_____
_____
_____
_____
_____
_____
_____
_____
_____
_____
_____
_____
_____

God, my prayer today is...

_____
_____
_____
_____
_____
_____

Enjoy!

He will take delight in you with gladness.

ZEPHANIAH 3:17 NLT

THERE'S ONE VERY HAPPY OBJECTIVE IN LIFE that many of us seem to struggle with: Enjoyment! Romans 14:17 CSB even says that the kingdom of heaven is "righteousness, peace, and *joy in the Holy Spirit.*" When we enjoy life, we are bringing God's kingdom to earth! So why is it so hard sometimes?

After all, we're meant to live with God's peace, trusting Him the way a baby trusts that her parents will hold her and love her and take care of her needs. God enjoys us. He really does! And since we are made in His image, we're designed to enjoy our own lives as His children. So please, give yourself permission to just spend time smiling. Hang out with friends who encourage, challenge, and love you for who you are. Make eye contact with others. Spend time outdoors. Get super excited when your favorite movie franchise releases the next trailer. Surprise your spouse with a gourmet meal. Serve your neighborhood widow, homeless shelter, or small business.

Yes, life has "downs"—but it also has "ups"—lots of them! And isn't a roller coaster, with all its dips and climbs, meant to exhilarate? This is your one chance to revel in the beauty of every drop of good life the Lord has chosen just for you.

Is enjoyment hard or easy for you?

_____

_____

_____

_____

_____

_____

_____

_____

_____

_____

_____

_____

Father, my prayer today is...

_____

_____

_____

_____

_____

_____

_____

Not So Ordinary

*Live in harmony with each other. Don't be too proud
to enjoy the company of ordinary people.*

ROMANS 12:16 NLT

THE BIBLE ENCOURAGES US not to compete for power, position, or influence or to seek the recognition and approval of people the world thinks are "important" (or try to become those people ourselves). The truth is, we are all important to God; each of us is special to Him. Each of us was created by Him to live forever with Him. As C. S. Lewis puts it, "There are no ordinary people. You have never talked to a mere mortal."

Now, not everybody knows it—or acts like it! But what a difference it makes when we do know how special we are to God, when we do act like it—when we live as if it matters, as if we matter. Because we do. And what an impact we can have when we treat others as special, when we show them they matter too.

Is there anyone on your heart to pray for this morning?

_____

_____

_____

_____

_____

_____

_____

_____

_____

_____

_____

_____

_____

God, my prayer today is...

_____

_____

_____

_____

_____

_____

_____

Need Directions?

Come near to God and He will come near to you.

JAMES 4:8 NIV

WHEN WE'RE BORN, we're all on the same page, starting from scratch, and growing as we go. We all fall down, get up, and start over. We find success in different things, we fail at different things, and we each have a beautiful, unique purpose that no one else has in quite the same way. Your journey is all yours, friend. Only God holds the map.

But you can find confidence in this: There are people praying for you. Jesus Himself is before the throne of the Father, speaking on your behalf. Your prayers matter to Him. He's the only One who really, truly knows how you feel. And He will be the first to tell you, whatever season you're in is just a season. It all serves His purpose as we draw close to Him. As we learn to trust Him, we will grow and mature, being enriched and blessed by God in ways beyond anything we can imagine right now.

Is there an area of life where you could use a little direction?

_____
_____
_____
_____
_____
_____
_____
_____
_____
_____
_____
_____
_____
_____

Father, my prayer today is...

_____
_____
_____
_____
_____
_____
_____

Designed in Detail

He counts the number of the stars;
He gives names to all of them.

PSALM 147:4 CSB

YOU, MY FRIEND, WERE METICULOUSLY DESIGNED by the Creator of the universe. He formulated your DNA down to the last twist. He programmed your body type, likes and dislikes, gifts and talents, and so much more. You were built from the ground up by the most magnificent mechanic, and as you follow Him, you are becoming the very person He created you to be. He champions your strengths, loves you through your weaknesses, and constantly whispers in your direction so that you will always be able to find Him.

God designed the color of your eyes to go with the shape of your face. He appointed that smile, those fingers, that wisp of hair. Instead of worrying, spend your time marveling at the creation you see in the mirror. And marvel at the fact that God is asking you to partner with Him to live your very best life.

You were chosen by God, loved by Him, and designed in great detail. He knew your name before you were even a thought in your parents' mind.

What is the story of the name you were given at birth?

_____

_____

_____

_____

_____

_____

_____

_____

_____

_____

_____

_____

_____

Father, my prayer today is...

_____

_____

_____

_____

_____

_____

Those Hidden Seasons

Make it your goal to live a quiet life,
minding your own business and working with your hands.

I THESSALONIANS 4:11 NLT

LET'S FACE IT, MOST OF LIFE isn't those exhilarating, top-of-the-world moments. A vast majority of our days involve routine: laundry, food, texts and phone calls, housework, and regular work, and marriage work. There are bound to be days when you long for more than what your current life offers.

There were eighteen years or so of Jesus's life about which little is written. Between His time teaching at the temple at twelve years old and the beginning of His ministry at thirty years old, we only have one verse to tell us what happened in that span of time. Luke 2:52 NLT says that "Jesus grew in wisdom and in stature and in favor with God and all the people." Jesus grew. He was a son, a brother. He lived a normal life. Learned his father's trade.

Mundane doesn't mean your life has no purpose. Small and quiet are not death sentences to your dreams and passions. Instead, those words are simply a different framework in which God is doing His work. This hidden season is fertile ground for Him to strip away what might be tainting our character, to heal our wounds and brokenness, and most importantly, to tell us again and again that our purpose, our worth, our identity aren't found in accomplishments. Our worth is found in being loved by God, our identity is grounded in Christ, and our purpose is to be like Him.

Do you find joy in the mundane, or does it feel tedious to you?

_____
_____
_____
_____
_____
_____
_____
_____
_____
_____
_____
_____
_____

God, my prayer today is...

_____
_____
_____
_____
_____
_____

Invest Well

*I chose you. I appointed you to go and produce fruit
and that your fruit should remain.*

JOHN 15:16 CSB

IN MATTHEW 25:14-30, the master of the house entrusted three servants with his money while he went away on business. When the master returned, he praised the servants who made wise and thoughtful decisions with his money. He was upset when one servant made a foolish decision out of fear. We don't really know what went on while the master was gone. But for the servants who made wise decisions, they must have invested. They must have spent time researching good options, thinking them through, and keeping tabs on the money. They treated their master's treasure as though it were their own.

Believe it or not, God trusts you! He has given you one life to do with as you see fit. You will likely face fear, and you will definitely face many decisions. But God has empowered you to live wisely and wildly, loving all that He has given you to steward and allowing Him to lead the way. Invest well, and your life will succeed.

If life is a garden, then you are the gardener. You have no control over the power within the seeds. But you can help the seeds tap into their power. As you nurture life, water and feed it, and live face-to-the-Son, good fruit will most certainly grow.

*What are some areas of life
that you are cultivating right now?*

_____
_____
_____
_____
_____
_____
_____
_____
_____
_____
_____
_____
_____
_____

Lord, my prayer today is...

_____
_____
_____
_____
_____
_____
_____

Good All Around

Taste and see that the LORD is good.

PSALM 34:8 CSB

GOD'S GOODNESS is in the slow cooker in fall, with its sliced vegetables and sizzling meat, delicious spices, and the promise of a warm meal on a chilly evening. In a world that holds tables to gather around, family to break bread with, and meals to be made, there is good.

God's goodness is in the laundry pile, with its whites and bright colors and the *swish-swash* of the washer. There's goodness in the *whoosh* of the vacuum as it cleans up dog hair and crumbs from games played and snacks enjoyed. There's goodness in stacking books on shelves and going to the store for shampoo and bananas. There's goodness in checking in with family via texts, keeping the calendars up-to-date, and placing books on hold at the library.

God, who loves us as much today as He did on day one, makes all things work for the good of those who love Him. He thinks of us constantly, more than grains of sand could number. He went to the grave and back for me and you. There is good all over the world. Walking to school. A thought-provoking sermon at church. Fresh-fallen snow. The crisp pages of a new, blank journal. A hot latte. A letter from a friend. Daisies growing in a sidewalk crack.

Goodness isn't hard to find, especially when you're on the lookout. May you see the goodness of the Lord, right there in your everyday.

Find three things within sight, taste, hearing, touch,
or smell that you consider good.

_____

_____

_____

_____

_____

_____

_____

_____

_____

_____

_____

_____

_____

Lord, my prayer today is...

_____

_____

_____

_____

_____

_____

Slow and Still

Be still, and know that I am God; I will be exalted.

PSALM 46:10 NIV

WHEN GOD REMINDED US in Psalm 46:10 to be still, that came with a second command: to know. The Hebrew word for "know" in this verse is *yadá*, which also means "to feel." *Be still*, God says, *and feel that I am God. Let it sink into your bones—this knowledge, this awareness, that I AM.*

As you start this day, take a moment to stop and close your eyes, take a deep breath, and remember God. Consider this day. All that it could hold, and all that it holds already. All that God has called you into, and the fact that He promises to be there with you every step of the way.

There will be times when you're sad. Be still and feel the sadness. Turn your thoughts toward the Creator of feelings, and know that He's not offended at your tears. In the moments when you are overjoyed, turn your glee in His direction and thank Him profusely. Then be still and soak in the light of that joy.

As often as you think of it, slow everything down and remember God—when you need Him most, and when you think you need Him least. Even as we go for a run or have a dance party, we can be still before God and enjoy this life He's given us...one feeling at a time.

*As you pause and take that deep breath,
what does God bring your attention to this morning?*

_____
_____
_____
_____
_____
_____
_____
_____
_____
_____
_____
_____
_____
_____
_____

Lord, my prayer today is...

_____
_____
_____
_____
_____
_____
_____

You're Covered

Whoever dwells in the shelter of the Most High
will rest in the shadow of the Almighty.
I will say of the LORD, "He is my refuge
and my fortress, my God, in whom I trust."

PSALM 91:1-2 NIV

LIFE IS FULL OF CHANGE. Some change—like getting a raise or suddenly becoming the championship team in your league—is pretty easy to handle. Other change can shake us up pretty badly. But the best news is that God does NOT change. He is the one constant through it all, supporting you and loving you exactly the same no matter what. He's not impressed by fame or fortune. He's also not intimidated by a scary diagnosis or a broken relationship. If you continue to trust and take it one day at a time, you will find that His hand never did let go of yours.

Psalm 91 is a resource for anyone who needs reminding. David experienced the highest of highs (think of killing a giant and saving a nation) and the lowest of lows (as a murderer and conspirator whose firstborn son died in infancy). He learned through his life to cry out to God in need and to declare the truth of who God really is. Psalm 91 declares those truths and promises. When you feel alone and overwhelmed, consider turning there and remembering what is true.

Read Psalm 91. What is your favorite line?

_____
_____
_____
_____
_____
_____
_____
_____
_____
_____
_____
_____
_____
_____

God, my prayer today is...

_____
_____
_____
_____
_____
_____
_____

A Way Forward

He will not let you stumble; the one who
watches over you will not slumber.

PSALM 121:3 NLT

EACH MORNING, you tie up your laces and step outside. Your feet pound the pavement as you try to relieve the pressure that presses from the inside. You are out of breath before you make it to the end of the block. You battle your thoughts. Just go home! You could curl back up under the covers for another hour. But there's a voice inside of you saying, *No, you need this. Stay the course. You'll find your rhythm. It will get easier. Just breathe.*

Sanity is a good thing. You turn toward the foothills aglow with morning light and make your way to the quaint Main Street just coming alive. Shop owners turn on lights, hot coffee pots steam as waitresses in maroon aprons fill mugs for customers huddled around small sidewalk tables. You keep pushing north.

Each morning, every single person has a unique day before them. Some days feel mundane, with no surprises ahead. Other days promise big things in big ways. And then there are those days that come after sleepless nights of worry. But no matter what, each day comes with a way forward. Some days feel like slogging with all you've got. But friend, know that every step forward is a victory. Every moment, you are living the life God designed you for. Keep pressing on.

What does this day promise to hold for you?

_____
_____
_____
_____
_____
_____
_____
_____
_____
_____
_____
_____
_____
_____

Father, my prayer today is...

_____
_____
_____
_____
_____
_____

The Words We Say

I lavish unfailing love for a thousand generations
on those who love Me and obey My commands.

EXODUS 20:6 NLT

THE WORDS WE SAY are like valuable little nuggets that others can treasure. Each one is unique. It costs very little. Once you say something, you don't hold onto it. The kind word is there for the other to pick up and tuck somewhere special in their heart to unwrap over and over again—reminding themselves of the beautiful truth of who they are.

Every person on the planet is constantly bombarded with words. Some are true, some not so true—but every word has impact. You get to choose how you build others up in important and unique ways. You might wonder if it means anything to be kind to an utter stranger, or to someone who gets under your skin, or to that person who appears not to be listening. But Isaiah 55:11 should encourage you: It's a promise that every word from God—every true word that is meant to encourage or strengthen another person in Christ—has value. It never doesn't matter! Another thing you can do is write a note or pass a card along, giving them something they can go back to when they're feeling more receptive. You never know the impact your words will have in God's perfect timing.

*What was a kind, important, or encouraging message
someone had for you recently?*

_____
_____
_____
_____
_____
_____
_____
_____
_____
_____
_____
_____
_____

God, my prayer today is...

_____
_____
_____
_____
_____
_____

Yes, You

See what great love the Father has lavished on us,
that we should be called children of God!

1 JOHN 3:1 NIV

GOD SEES YOUR ROLE on this earth as a valuable calling. In His wisdom, He has gifted you individually. He delights in you personally. He has paired you and prepared you, equipped you and called you, dressed you in His finest armor to face the day with joy. You have no idea how much you influence your world.

God. Delights. In. You. Yep, you. You, who are weary. You, who are not a parent to children of your blood. You, in the office cubicle. You, who diligently serve on church committees or in community groups. You, who love being a parent. You are beloved to Him. God delights in His children. The end.

When you feel the weight of not knowing whether you make a difference. When you feel the tedium of another day. When you feel the heat of trying to do the very best you can. God sees it all, and reassures you: *Count it all joy, child. I see you. I know you. I can't wait for you to feel the warmth of my acceptance in all its fullness. In the meantime, take comfort in the peace that passes understanding. You are right where you belong—in this home, in this life, and in My heart.*

When you are doing something that makes you feel
most fulfilled, what is it you're doing?

_____
_____
_____
_____
_____
_____
_____
_____
_____
_____
_____
_____
_____

Lord, my prayer today is...

_____
_____
_____
_____
_____
_____
_____

Bless Them

*I will bless you and make your descendants
into a great nation. You will become famous
and be a blessing to others.*

GENESIS 12:2 CEV

THERE'S EVIDENCE all over the Old and New Testaments that blessing others with our mouths and hearts is a regular practice in the kingdom of God. But what does that mean exactly? Sometimes we think of blessings as tangible things. "This new car is a real blessing." "I'll ask God to bless you with good health." But in reality, a blessing is more accurately a pronunciation of happiness or an act of praise. God's blessings bring happiness to us, and we can pronounce a wish of happiness over others. God is also blessed when we praise Him.

It may seem strange to bless someone when they're out of earshot. But when we bless, we aren't necessarily speaking to their minds. We are spiritual beings, after all. A blessing, delivered on the wings of the Holy Spirit is a gift to the spirit of a person. You have the ability to pronounce happiness over your neighbor, grocer, police officer, or family member whether they're in the room with you or not. When you bless someone, it blesses your own heart too. If you have an unkind interchange with a fellow driver, for example, practice blessing them and then check the status of your own heart. Chances are, you'll feel much better than if you had chosen to curse them out for their driving choices.

Every word of kindness and happiness that you speak over someone else will take root. It will grow and bear fruit. We don't always know how that fruit will manifest—but your words, without a doubt, will have a positive effect.

Do you find it hard or easy to bless someone you disagree with?

_____

_____

_____

_____

_____

_____

_____

_____

_____

_____

_____

_____

_____

God, my prayer today is...

_____

_____

_____

_____

_____

_____

Joining Forces

A cord of three strands is not easily broken.

ECCLESIASTES 4:12 CSB

L ET'S FACE IT. If you've been married for at least twelve minutes, you know that disagreements with your spouse will happen. There's so much new and unknown in joining forces with another human being. You've had different upbringings and experiences. And as much as you might discuss life philosophies and goals before and during marriage, putting them into practice is a whole different ordeal.

In the 2020 NFL season, Tom Brady was playing quarterback for the Tampa Bay Buccaneers after twenty seasons with the New England Patriots. As a Patriot, Brady had won six Super Bowls and multiple MVP awards, so hopes were high for the Buccaneers at the start of 2020. But the first game of the season did not go well. It wasn't that Brady had become a bad player overnight. But he was on a new team, running plays he'd never run with teammates he'd never been in a game with before. It would take time, effort, and learning for him to connect well with a whole new team.

You and your spouse are constantly running plays you've never run before. No matter how incredible your problem-solving, communication, and relationship skills are, life is so good at throwing curveballs. But in the end, you can be confident that you are meant to be a team and that with practice, you'll get the win.

*Single or married, what is an area of marriage
you think needs the most prayer?*

_____

_____

_____

_____

_____

_____

_____

_____

_____

_____

_____

_____

_____

_____

God, my prayer today is...

_____

_____

_____

_____

_____

_____

_____

When You're Worried

I can do everything through Christ, who gives me strength.

PHILIPPIANS 4:13 NLT

EVERYWHERE WE LOOK, we can find things worth worrying about. It's been said that worry is what happens when we don't trust our future to God. But with Him, everything seems to work out.

Everything—from fevers to feelings, the nightly news to no news at all—becomes an opportunity for worry. It's only through time and trust, experience and prayer, that we walk through it all, little by little, and learn. If you are prone to worry, here are a few Scriptures that can help. Look them up, memorize them, or just take them to heart when you need them most.

> "When you lie down, you will not be afraid; when you lie down, your sleep will be sweet." (Proverbs 3:24 NIV)

> "Seek first His kingdom and His righteousness, and all these things will be given to you as well." (Matthew 6:33 NIV)

> "Look, I am making everything new!" (Revelation 21:5 NLT)

> "He will feed His flock like a shepherd; He will gather the lambs with His arm...and gently lead those who are with young." (Isaiah 40:11 NKJV)

A quick Google search will help you find so many more Scriptures leading to peace and fearlessness. Most importantly, always remember that God is with you. He is for you. He loves you more than you can imagine, sees you when no one else does, and cares for you with His whole heart.

When you worry, what is your go-to Scripture verse?
What does it mean to you?

_____
_____
_____
_____
_____
_____
_____
_____
_____
_____
_____
_____
_____
_____

Father, my prayer today is...

_____
_____
_____
_____
_____
_____
_____

A Legacy of Your Own

You shall expand to the right and to the left,
and your descendants will inherit the nations.

ISAIAH 54:3 NKJV

THE HISTORY OF ABUSE, pain, and confusion from Shawna's childhood was enough to make her worry about raising healthy children. Could she impart pure love to her daughter when her own childhood was full of trauma? She was advised by a pastor friend to pour out her concerns to God and then leave them at His feet. When times were hard, she prayed and carried His peace. The best part is, Shawna no longer worries that her daughter will carry on a legacy of destruction in the ways that her family did. The cycle is broken.

Derek's grandfather started a heating and cooling company in the 1920s. Derek would toddle around the storefront as a boy while his dad and grandpa worked in the machine shop and his mom helped customers. He loved growing up in a family that worked together, but when he went to college, he decided to take a different path from the family business. His degree in psychology and a satisfying marketing career have little to do with the small shop his grandfather started. But from his family, Derek learned important values: hard work, together time, adapting to change, and showing excellence and kindness toward people. Derek defines his career and family life as successful.

Whatever your legacy—the Lord will lead you in passing on the good and healing from the bad. When you lean, He leads. That's a promise.

What is a positive trait you see in yourself
that you got from a parent or grandparent?

_____
_____
_____
_____
_____
_____
_____
_____
_____
_____
_____
_____
_____
_____

Lord, my prayer today is...

_____
_____
_____
_____
_____
_____

Never Alone

*I pray that you, being rooted and firmly established in love,
may be able to comprehend with all the saints
what is the length and width, height and depth of God's love.*

EPHESIANS 3:17–18 CSB

THROUGHOUT LIFE WE FIND OURSELVES in new and unknown situations. It can be a lot like the first day of school—clinging to Mama's pant leg as we step timidly into some place we've never been, wondering if it's safe, wondering if we'll make friends and have fun and like what they serve for snacks.

Depending on the day, we may feel like we've been abandoned to fend for ourselves. As God's beloved children, though, we are never on the brink of abandonment, despite what our feelings tell us. In fact, even though we feel like God has left and He's out of our sight (especially when we veer off His prescribed path), His sovereign hand is still holding us. Before the world was even created, God devised a plan through faith in His Son that would pave a permanent path back to Him no matter what problem besets us.

One of the reasons God wants a relationship with us is so that, in moments of fear or panic, we become accustomed to turning inward toward His voice and comfort. He's always there, with a pant leg we can cling to. Our loving Father, our heavenly Daddy, has made a way for us to belong to Him forever, and He will never leave us, nor will He forsake us.

Write about a time you felt God's hands holding you.

_____

_____

_____

_____

_____

_____

_____

_____

_____

_____

_____

_____

_____

_____

_____

Father, my prayer today is...

_____

_____

_____

_____

_____

_____

_____

His Strong and Tender Arms

*He tends His flock like a shepherd: He gathers
the lambs in His arms and carries them close to His heart;
He gently leads those that have young.*

ISAIAH 40:11 NIV

ISAIAH 40, VERSE 10, describes God coming with power and His mighty arm. Then, in verse 11, that same strong arm is used to gently swoop us up and carry us so tenderly. Everything we need from a perfect Father and powerful Shepherd, we can find in God.

A mama sheep, when she sees a stranger, will immediately start guarding her babies and bleating. She will protect her young from danger—but soften entirely when the familiar farmer comes. The sheer sound of his voice will put her at ease. She knows she is safe. She will even allow him close to her most treasured possessions, her babies.

Jesus is our Good Shepherd. His sheep know His voice. He gently cares for His young. He protects and guides them. He nourishes them. As His followers, we can be sure that He is perfectly leading us. There's no need to fear that we aren't enough. We can relax in Jesus, knowing we're guarded and watched over.

What does it mean to you to think of God with both
a mighty arm and one that gently carries you?

_____
_____
_____
_____
_____
_____
_____
_____
_____
_____
_____
_____
_____
_____
_____

God, my prayer today is...

_____
_____
_____
_____
_____
_____
_____

Growing Great

For I am confident of this very thing,
that He who began a good work among you
will complete it by the day of Christ Jesus.

PHILIPPIANS 1:6 NASB

AS YOU WAKE UP THIS MORNING, know this: You are doing great. No...really. These aren't just some words on a printed page meant for many people. These words are just for you. Because if you're reading this, you're obviously interested in growing in faith and in life.

If you know Jesus, then you are on a one-of-a-kind journey. You've put yourself in His hands, to break you down where needed and build you up even stronger than before. You've received the gift of the Holy Spirit, at work in you to shape you into someone looking more and more like Jesus Himself. As you press in, listening for His voice, surrendering yourself and your loved ones to Him, releasing fears and problems into His hands, you are going down a path that will perfect you. You are a new creation spiritually!

God has the whole picture, and He knows exactly where you fit. It's completely normal to feel inadequate at times. But Jesus lifts you up, strengthens you, and makes the impossible, well, fun! You're definitely growing. Fortunately, it's impossible to outgrow Jesus. You need Him now, and you'll need Him next year. You'll need Him on the best of days and on the grumpy ones, through all the ups and downs of living and loving. You need Him on this journey...and He's not going anywhere. He will continue to do good work in you until the day of Christ Jesus.

How do you hope to grow today?

_____
_____
_____
_____
_____
_____
_____
_____
_____
_____
_____
_____
_____

Lord, my prayer today is...

_____
_____
_____
_____
_____
_____
_____

Life Moves Fast

This is the day the LORD has made;
let's rejoice and be glad in it.

PSALM 118:24 CSB

BEFORE YOU KNOW IT, you'll look back and wonder where the time went. It will all seem like such a flash. Amid all the motivated Mondays and selfie-worthy Saturdays will be the ordinary, everyday days. The ones where you get up, get ready, go to work or the store or the living room—and nothing major happens. You'll have quiet times, and loud times, and belly laughs, and torrential tears. What seems huge today will be distant tomorrow, as new views and new adventures await. Every season of life carries its own challenges...but each one will fly. The very best thing to do is to savor every moment as much as you can. Relish the sweet times and rowdy times; the hard, grumpy times and the tender, emotional ones. Because simply having those times means that you have breath in your lungs and a beat in your heart—gifts from the Lord, truly.

And you know what? You've got this; the Lord is on your side. There is no need to be afraid. God has gifted this life to you, and He will never leave you to do it all alone. Your reward is in heaven. While you can't know the full effect you are having on the world around you each day, the efforts you are making do not go unnoticed by your heavenly Father. He loves you so much. So love on. Pray on. Heaven is going to be such an incredible revelation.

How will you treasure your time today?

_____
_____
_____
_____
_____
_____
_____
_____
_____
_____
_____
_____
_____
_____

Father, my prayer today is...

_____
_____
_____
_____
_____
_____

The Way of Love

God will tenderly comfort you....
He will give you the strength to endure.

II CORINTHIANS 1:7 TLB

LOVING PEOPLE can be such a challenge. There will be times that you wish had never happened. There will be days that you want to do over. There will be moments when you think to yourself, *I'm not strong enough for this*. It's the way of love. To care so deeply for others, we have to accept that there will be heartbreak along with the incredible gift of closeness with those you love.

But here's where God's design comes with a release valve. According to the Bible, the Holy Spirit is our Comforter (John 14:26 KJV). Although pain is inevitable in relationships, the comfort of God is just as inevitable. His promise is strong. He will carry you in times of sorrow. His wisdom will guide you through the hardest times. His own love for you will shelter and surround you at all times. And with His comfort, you'll come out stronger than before.

Having close relationships means that there will be incredibly happy times as well as difficult times. There's so much that only time and experience can shed light on. But the Bible is full of promises for all times and situations. When you need God most, He will be there. You can turn to His promises for all seasons. And when you need it, His comfort will get you through.

List a few of the people that have made your life richer
and better, despite some of the challenges of loving them.

_____
_____
_____
_____
_____
_____
_____
_____
_____
_____
_____
_____
_____
_____

Lord, my prayer today is...

_____
_____
_____
_____
_____
_____
_____

Schedule Some Margin

He has shown you, O man, what is good;
and what does the LORD require of you but to do justly,
to love mercy, and to walk humbly with your God?

MICAH 6:8 NKJV

HAVE YOU EVER NOTICED that almost any job or activity can take up the entire amount of time you give it? In other words, margin is not created by accident. We need to actually look for, and sometimes fight for, that extra space in our days and lives to breathe. Margin is something we must schedule, prioritize, and treat just as seriously as our activities. Sometimes we worry that if we do make way for this intentional time of solitude, stillness, or room to "just be," we will compromise our other areas of attention. However, what we don't realize, until it's too late, is that if we do not demand margin from ourselves, the other areas of our life will naturally suffer.

By allowing ourselves to have true free time, our heart remembers what we naturally enjoy. We are far more inclined to take a walk around the neighborhood, read an inspiring book, or get back our green thumb. Our passion is reignited and we give ourselves space to think, to receive instruction from God, to learn more about our gifts, and to remember the purpose behind this whole thing called life. Any time we spend with God doing whatever it is that we love to do is never wasted. We become more efficient employees, more compassionate friends, more patient parents, more respectful romantic partners, and more intentional, aware people.

Is there any margin scheduled into your day today?
Can you find some space for it right now?

_____

_____

_____

_____

_____

_____

_____

_____

_____

_____

_____

_____

_____

_____

Father, my prayer today is...

_____

_____

_____

_____

_____

_____

No FOMO

*Every good gift and every perfect gift is from above,
and comes down from the Father.*

JAMES 1:17 NKJV

IT HAPPENS TO THE BEST OF US: FOMO. Fear of Missing Out. Somehow we feel that where we are in life is not where everyone else seems to be, and we think we're the only one not invited to the party. One of the most beautiful things about life in Jesus is that our life with Him is as rich and amazing and full and wonderful as anyone could ever hope for. Even the hard stuff. Because He works ALL things together for your good. Really, the very best thing we can do daily is to slow down and enjoy right where we are. Maybe—just maybe—it's not us missing out but the rest of the world.

Maybe the world needs to sit down, take a breath, lean back into God's arms, and find comfort there. Maybe the world has forgotten how to relish life. Maybe you and your friendship with the Creator of the universe are the stuff of envy. And maybe the world knows it. Maybe the world will try to convince you to be more like it, when you have every right to whisper from your morning table with your cup of coffee and open Bible, "Come sit. Enjoy this moment. Really, really enjoy it. Don't let it slip past unnoticed."

How often do you experience FOMO? How do you handle it?

_____

_____

_____

_____

_____

_____

_____

_____

_____

_____

_____

_____

_____

_____

_____

_____

Lord, my prayer today is...

_____

_____

_____

_____

_____

_____

Mighty Warrior

Be ready! Let the truth be like a belt around your waist, and let God's justice protect you like armor. Your desire to tell the good news about peace should be like shoes on your feet. Let your faith be like a shield, and you will be able to stop all the flaming arrows of the evil one. Let God's saving power be like a helmet, and for a sword use God's message that comes from the Spirit.

EPHESIANS 6:14–17 CEV

THE BATTLE IS FIERCE, but you are not hopeless, helpless, or defenseless. God has equipped you with everything you need to fight and win! He has given you spiritual "armor" to protect you. And faith, hope, courage, strength, grace, truth, love—these are just a few of the powerful weapons with which God has equipped you—not to mention peace, patience, endurance, and so many others. With these weapons, you can overcome fear and doubt; you can defeat discouragement and despair. You can persevere in righteousness (right living) and making wise choices. You can not only survive but thrive in the most difficult challenges of your life. God has made you a mighty warrior, and He is for you!

What do you feel equipped to do today?

_____
_____
_____
_____
_____
_____
_____
_____
_____
_____
_____
_____
_____
_____

God, my prayer today is...

_____
_____
_____
_____
_____
_____
_____

Childlike Faith

We put our hope in the LORD.
He is our help and our shield.

PSALM 33:20 NLT

WHETHER THEY REALIZE IT OR NOT, babies trust their caregivers. Let's say you've had a little boy. He doesn't worry about being fed, changed, or snuggled. He doesn't consider whether it's a good idea to suck on the dog's squeaky toy, or whether it's safe to climb the nearest chair and reach for an object high on a shelf. A baby trusts his parents to be there no matter what. And often, he doesn't even see the danger he could be in. He gets upset that something is taken away from him. He is so caught up in his moment—discovering and exploring—that it takes a more experienced eye to guide his process. In fact, it's his childlike faith in his parents and protectors that allows him to live freely and discover the world around him.

As adults, we are invited into a childlike faith. Our heavenly Father takes on the role of our protector and shepherd. He sees our surroundings and knows what is best for us. And we can rely on Him to keep us secure in Him as we adventure through this life.

Just as your baby boy will turn to you when he recognizes the need, we can turn to God as often as we need. He is our shield, our help, and our most trustworthy Father. And He wants nothing more than to love us with His everlasting love.

What new adventures would you like to explore
if you felt completely secure in God's care?

_____
_____
_____
_____
_____
_____
_____
_____
_____
_____
_____
_____
_____
_____
_____

Lord, my prayer today is...

_____
_____
_____
_____
_____
_____
_____

Friends for the Deep End

That's how it is with us. There are many of us,
but we each are part of the body of Christ,
as well as part of one another.

ROMANS 12:5 CEV

WE'RE NOT DESIGNED TO DO LIFE ALONE. We're designed for community. There are days when all we need is for someone to look us in the eyes and say, "Me too, friend. Can I pray for you?" Or show up in joggers and a tank top just to share a cup of coffee and a laugh.

You might be craving the companionship of others with whom you can walk this path. There's just something about facing similar situations, fears, and celebrations in the same moment with people who really see you. If this is you, then pray, "Lord Jesus, please bring me friends." And He will.

In between the shared experiences, prayer times, silly moments and serious ones, friendship will form. Jesus-joined hearts will grow stronger together. Because that's what friendship does. We were never meant to travel this life without the refuge of friends.

Life lived in relationships allows us to survive the deep end. We can test the waters alone, wade out a bit by ourselves, but if we must head to the deep places of life, we need friends to keep the ocean from swallowing us whole. Each friendship can serve as a line, tethering us to the shore when life tries to suck us under. In His great mercy and grace, our Jesus has given us the gift of friendship.

In what ways can you build and foster new friendships today?

_____
_____
_____
_____
_____
_____
_____
_____
_____
_____
_____
_____
_____
_____

God, my prayer today is...

_____
_____
_____
_____
_____
_____
_____

Live in Joy

The lines have fallen to me in pleasant places;
Yes, I have a good inheritance.

PSALM 16:6 NKJV

IN THE BOOK OF NEHEMIAH, the Israelites had tried for years to rebuild the walls of Jerusalem, with no success. Nehemiah was finally able to orchestrate the rebuild. And on the day the people gathered to celebrate, Ezra read Scripture publicly. The people heard all the ways they'd fallen short of God's glory. They wanted to mourn and grieve. But Ezra commanded them not to. He reminded them that it was a day of celebration and asked the people to see the joy of the Lord as their strength (Nehemiah 8:10). Ezra knew that wallowing in their own shortcomings would solve nothing. Instead, he counted on God's joy to sustain them. Calling on joy would cause them to think more like God, serving those who were in need.

Living in joy allows us to see life through God's eyes. Where comparing and envy keep us from moving forward—joy lets us leap. Joy allows us to love the people we're with. Joy looks past dust or dirty dishes and sees the home that keeps us safe. Joy is what ultimately shines through our online posts, making people wonder what makes our family different even though our circumstances may not be picture-perfect.

If you're going to make comparisons, then compare yourself to where you were a year ago—who you were before you kicked that bad habit or chose that new good habit. Compare life to a few years ago and ask yourself if you're headed in the right direction. Then grab onto the joy, and keep on going.

What is one way you've grown in the past year?

_____
_____
_____
_____
_____
_____
_____
_____
_____
_____
_____
_____
_____
_____
_____

Lord, my prayer today is...

_____
_____
_____
_____
_____
_____
_____

In the Quiet

The LORD your God is with you....
He will take great delight in you...
He will...rejoice over you with singing.

ZEPHANIAH 3:17 NIV

IT'S BEEN A LONG DAY. Not a bad one, to be sure. With all the busyness and activities, relationships to maintain, issues to deal with, and new things to celebrate...the day has just gotten away from you. And now, for the first time, you are coming into a quiet moment. The house is peaceful and the lights are dim. You sit in a comfortable chair and just breathe. It's easier, at this moment, to remind yourself that God is in charge. That the story has an ending, and the ending is good! It seems so natural to smile as you hum along to your favorite songs without a care in the world.

Perhaps it seems so natural because it's exactly how your Father in heaven treats you. He has such tenderness for you. Not that everything we do delights Him. But He sees us as His children —unwise to all the world's ways, vulnerable in emotion, and doing our best with what we've been given. A mother wouldn't berate her toddler for falling down while learning to run, any more than God would punish us for doing our best and falling short.

In the quiet of the night, when you can turn off the worries and busyness, a still, small voice comes through. It's the voice of love. It's the one that softly hums, gently rocks your spirit against His chest, and quietly whispers that He's proud of who you are and all that you are becoming.

What songs are speaking to you right now?
What lyrics bring you comfort?

_____
_____
_____
_____
_____
_____
_____
_____
_____
_____
_____
_____
_____

God, my prayer today is...

_____
_____
_____
_____
_____
_____
_____

Showing Up and Lifting Up

Encourage one another.

1 THESSALONIANS 5:11 NIV

IF YOU'VE EVER DONE a 5K (3.1-mile) walk or run in your community, you've probably found it pretty encouraging. Depending on the race and the reason for it, you're in a crowd of energized people on a common mission: Get to the finish line. For fun. They may be dressed in colorful costumes or tutus. They may be in groups, or wearing shirts supporting friends with breast cancer. They may be pushing strollers. They may be dressed in their military uniforms and carrying flags. And most likely, if you say "Good job!" to them, they'll smile and say "You too!" with enthusiasm.

In a 5K, some people are in it to win, and some are in it to finish with a smile. Almost everyone has a story behind their jog. Some people run one in their lifetime and call it quits, while others collect finisher medals like they're candy. But the common ground is showing up, usually early on a Saturday morning, and following the same path to the finish line.

If life is a race, then we're all runners needing encouragement. We'll also benefit from lifting others up as we go. Because we were made to encourage. And wonderfully enough, encouraging others will fill us up too.

When was the last time you felt especially encouraged
by a gathering of like-minded people?

_____
_____
_____
_____
_____
_____
_____
_____
_____
_____
_____
_____
_____
_____

Father, my prayer today is...

_____
_____
_____
_____
_____
_____

You. Are. Enough.

We are God's handiwork, created in Christ Jesus
to do good works, which God prepared in advance for us to do.

EPHESIANS 2:10 NIV

SOCIAL MEDIA IS QUICK TO TELL US that we just don't measure up. By the look of people's homes and puppies, everyone else's lives are nearly perfect. As you scroll along, enviously noting their sunny vacations, intimate together times, masterfully plated meals, constantly clean clothes and well-behaved siblings—you glance over at your dish-coated sink and crumb-covered counter.

The truth is, people rarely memorialize their less-than-perfect times on their pages. And in much the same way, the world rarely sees the insecurities and worries we face every time we lay our head on the pillow at night. We judge others by their neatly trimmed outer lives, and we judge ourselves by our messy, disorganized, emotional insides. That, friend, is not apples to apples.

But the greater truth? You. Are. Enough. Sure—everyone can learn and grow. There may be books worth reading and experts worth following. There are friends or family members worth observing in their strengths. Scripture even tells us we need mentors. But that doesn't mean you're not exactly where you belong, right now, for this point in history.

Don't let anyone ever tell you that your life is less than. You were designed to pour into the world around you for God's glory. He prepared you and gives you everything you need, every day.

What is a special, unique gift or ability that you have?

_____
_____
_____
_____
_____
_____
_____
_____
_____
_____
_____
_____
_____
_____
_____
_____

Lord, my prayer today is...

_____
_____
_____
_____
_____
_____
_____
_____

Rest Assured

Now if any of you lacks wisdom, he should ask God —
who gives to all generously and ungrudgingly —
and it will be given to him.

JAMES 1:5 CSB

A S YOU OPEN YOUR EYES and prepare for this day, you can rest assured. Rest in the knowledge that God is in control. Rest in the awareness of the beauty and hope all around you. Rest, believing that nothing will come at you today that God hasn't known about, equipped you for, and considered your steps through. That's the joy of trusting Him: When you put on His full armor (Ephesians 6:10-18), you're more ready for the day than most of the people you'll meet!

An artist was once scoffed at for charging a large sum of money for his autograph. The scoffer said, "Signing your name took five seconds. How could you expect so much money for it?" The artist replied, "That signature took thirty years of practicing, sharing, and marketing my craft. You are not paying for ink on paper; you are paying for what it took to have you ask me for my signature."

In other words, your life to this moment has prepared you for whatever you'll face today. If you think you aren't ready, just ask! God promises to give you the wisdom you need. You've got years and years of experience and learning to pull from. The Lord will help you draw out whatever you already know and then fill in the gaps with grace. It's going to be a good day.

Read Ephesians 6:10-18. Which part of His armor is your favorite?

_____
_____
_____
_____
_____
_____
_____
_____
_____
_____
_____
_____
_____
_____
_____

Father, my prayer today is...

_____
_____
_____
_____
_____
_____

We Belong Together

Live in harmony with one another.

ROMANS 12:16 NIV

THE AFRICAN BUFFALO HAS A UNIQUE PRACTICE of deciding which way to travel. Individual females in the herd will stand up, look in a certain direction, then lie back down—almost as if they're voting. Majority wins. Elephants, too, are known to be socially complex. They live in families, with the adults cooperating to provide food, childcare, defense, and decision-making. And the female mule deer has a pact with other adult females. When she goes out hunting, she leaves her babies near another mama deer. If a predator comes, the babysitter mama will protect her own babies as well as the babies of the hunting mom.

Many other animal species seem to have an innate understanding for the importance of community. But humans also have the command to live that way. There are fifty-nine "one another" commands in the New Testament. Some of the commands include:

"Be at peace with one another." (Mark 9:50 CSB)

"Wash one another's feet." (John 13:14 CSB)

"Love one another." (John 13:34 CSB)

"Be devoted to one another in love." (Romans 12:10 NIV)

"Honor one another above yourselves." (Romans 12:10 NIV)

Do you think God was serious about making sure we know we belong together? And that we be together with respect and love for one another? We're designed for community. And we can trust God when He calls us into something. Inviting others into our lives has the potential to make life infinitely richer. It's a priceless gift to share the gift of life with other believers.

How does living in community enrich your life?

_____
_____
_____
_____
_____
_____
_____
_____
_____
_____
_____
_____
_____
_____

Lord, my prayer today is...

_____
_____
_____
_____
_____
_____

For Weary Travelers

He guides the humble in what is right
and teaches them His way.

PSALM 25:9 NIV

AT TIMES IN THE JOURNEY OF LIFE, you are likely to experience "weary traveler syndrome." You'll find yourself at a fork in the road, with no map or compass to confirm which way to go. You might feel stranded, abandoned, unprepared to take a step forward in any direction. What if you make the wrong decision? What if you change your mind? What if you're stuck and can't turn back? What if it's a disaster? What if you fail? You'll pile all the pros and cons and what-ifs into a mountain of anxious uncertainty.

Trying to discern what's best in the face of an ever-changing world can be so tough. That's why it's wonderful news to know that the world doesn't hinge on our ability to synthesize and analyze incomplete information, fill in every blank, and accurately predict the future. Nowhere does Scripture say, *Thou shalt make every decision perfectly and never make a mistake.* Because that's not God's heart for us. So what does Scripture say? God is with us.

"The LORD Himself goes before you and will be with you; He will never leave you nor forsake you. Do not be afraid; do not be discouraged" (Deuteronomy 31:8 NIV). God will guide you. Need more assurance that these things are true? Read Psalm 139. Then be honest with God about where you are. Tell Him if you feel alone or scared, lost or mad, or overwhelmed. Then rehearse the truth: "Even there Your hand will lead me; Your right hand will hold on to me" (Psalm 139:10 CSB).

The last time you were stuck in a decision,
how did you handle it?

_____
_____
_____
_____
_____
_____
_____
_____
_____
_____
_____
_____
_____
_____

Father, my prayer today is...

_____
_____
_____
_____
_____
_____

New Normals

I focus on this one thing....Looking forward to what lies ahead,
I press on to reach the end of the race.

PHILIPPIANS 3:13-14 NLT

WHEN YOU FIRST EXPERIENCE a transition in life, somewhere deep inside, you may begin with an attitude of "getting past this." You have a baby, but it won't be that different...will it? Or there's a job change, and naturally things will seem off-balance for a while. That diagnosis, that move, that breakup or commitment—every life change—changes everything...and it can happen all at once.

If you spent your entire young life living on the coast at sea level, you would be used to a certain fitness level. Maybe you're even a triathlete. Then you move to Denver, which has an altitude of over 5,000 feet. You learn very quickly that your body needs to adjust to the new altitude. You feel for a while like you are no longer an athlete. You pant when you jog. You tire quickly. But over time, your body adjusts to the new normal—and it actually makes you a stronger competitor when you travel back to your hometown on the coast!

New normals are a little like Denver. You're gasping for air, missing the ocean. You'll get glimpses of the past when you visit there, but it will never be the same. Your high-altitude home has caused you to change the way you live. But in the end, it will make you stronger and bring so much joy.

How has a major life change, or a minor one, affected your life?

_____

_____

_____

_____

_____

_____

_____

_____

_____

_____

_____

_____

_____

_____

Lord, my prayer today is...

_____

_____

_____

_____

_____

_____

_____

Look and Leap

*The Lord GOD is my strength [my source of courage,
my invincible army]; He has made my feet [steady and sure]
like hinds' feet and makes me walk [forward with spiritual
confidence] on my high places [of challenge and responsibility].*

HABAKKUK 3:19 AMP

YOU WERE MADE TO BE BEAUTIFUL AND STRONG, confident
and courageous, graceful and swift and agile—like a deer dancing across
the mountain heights. God Himself has created you to be everything you
need to be to live the life He's called you to and to fulfill His plans and
purposes for you.

Don't worry obsessively over the challenges and obstacles ahead of
you. Don't live in regret over past stumbles or tremble in fear while looking
down at the next steps. Don't look down at all. Look up! Lift your eyes and
look to Him. Trust Him. Draw your strength from His strength—and leap!

In what ways can you leap today?

_____
_____
_____
_____
_____
_____
_____
_____
_____
_____
_____
_____
_____
_____

God, my prayer today is...

_____
_____
_____
_____
_____
_____
_____

Soak It In

To everything there is a season,
a time for every purpose under heaven.

ECCLESIASTES 3:1 NKJV

SEASONS CHANGE. Depending on where you live, how they change may vary. But regardless, time is marked by a cycle of seasons that is inevitable.

Seasons feel different. In winter in the northern hemisphere, winter temperatures top out at a cooler number than in summer. Leaves on deciduous trees change colors, fall to the ground, stay dormant, and regrow in spring. Humidity marks the warmer temps in southern summers. Sheep, deer, cows, and other animals have their babies in the spring. Thanksgiving gives the fall a warm and cozy feel.

Seasons overlap. Although they have calendar dates to mark them, it's not like on March 21, every tulip blooms and every lamb is born. We might have snow in spring, and we might have hot weather in early fall. Dates just give us guidelines—a sense that a new season is coming.

How we handle our season says a lot about us, and says a lot about how we'll get through it. How often do we hear someone talking about sand and sea when it's 30 degrees and snowing? Or wishing for snow when the air conditioner breaks down? Instead of pining for greener grass, focus on thankfulness for the season you're in right now. You will get through every challenge. There will be smiles, laughter, tears, failures, parties, and sweet moments every step of the way. Soak up the season you're in, and look forward to whatever is next.

How would you describe your current season?

_____
_____
_____
_____
_____
_____
_____
_____
_____
_____
_____
_____
_____

Father, my prayer today is...

_____
_____
_____
_____
_____
_____
_____

The Seven-Minute Morning Journal: Inspiration for Your Quiet Time with God
Copyright © 2022 DaySpring Cards, Inc. All rights reserved.
First Edition, July 2022

Published by:

DaySpring

21154 Highway 16 East
Siloam Springs, AR 72761
dayspring.com

Written by: Trieste Vaillancourt
Cover Design by: Jason D. Kingsley

Printed in China
Prime: J8276
ISBN: 978-1-64870-633-2